HAPPY

Teaching The Craft of Writing Using Mentor Texts

WRITING

FRANCINA MAINER

Published by

M&L Media Publishing

Copyright © 2014 Francina Mainer

ISBN: 069228320X
ISBN-13: 9780692283202

DEDICATION

To my mentors both personal and professional

Who stood with me from the beginning of my career.

To my children, who have been on this journey with me since birth.

To my family and friends who encouraged me to share my gift.

CONTENTS

INTRODUCTION

"Success always occurs when preparation meets opportunity."

Henry Hartman

Writing well is long overdue at every grade and in every subject. It is not an option it is a necessity. As an educator, I have always known that being a successful reader is a predictor of being an excellent writer, and that prepares you to be an academic success. I am a reader and a writer that enjoys finding excellent literature to read and share with others especially teachers and students.

I have taught Elementary and Secondary Reading, Language Arts (English) and Writing for over thirty years in public schools, and have been a literacy coach for seven years. With both the range of experience and education that I have benefited from as an educator, I am at a point in my career that allows me to share the focus of my professional learning in writing to assist teachers and students become more successful.

Throughout my career I have seen students struggle with writing in all subjects. It became more profound to me when I became a literacy coach helping students and teachers in Kindergarten through Fifth grades that there is still a need for more professional learning of Writing.

Being a literacy coach, I partnered with teachers for professional learning that enhanced, strengthened, supported, and assisted teacher's reflections on students, the curriculum, and pedagogy for the purpose of more effective decision-making. Working in this role, as a literacy coach, has lead me to the passion I now have with helping teachers focus more of their attention on improving student achievement by working directly with them.

This book is written to assist teachers provide direct instruction to students, provide support for teachers in instructional decision making and developing the writing craft, using mentor texts and "mini lessons" to improve students' writing.

It became very apparent to me over fifteen years ago, while teaching writing to a fourth grade student, who had a difficult time with narrative writing that I needed support from administration or other colleagues, this student had difficulties with developing the beginning, middle, and the ending of the story. I did not receive any support from anyone, so I tried to think of a strategy that would work. I read to my class daily so on this day I continued to read the classic book, "Caps For Sale" by Esphyr Slobodkina. Suddenly, when it became time for our daily Writing Workshop, I had an epiphany moment, a strategy that would make an impact.

I decided to write down on the board some of the elements of the story from "Caps for Sale" like what was included in the beginning. I started with the Hook, Setting, Time, Problem and who the Characters were in the beginning of the story. I then asked students to brainstorm some different hooks, settings, times, problems, and characters. This idea was dynamic and it worked. I followed the same procedure for the middle and the end of the story. In fact, that student later passed the state writing test.

I am a true believer that you'll enjoy teaching writing when you read like a writer and when you read like a reader and make connections, visualize, infer, and question the mentor texts.

As an educator, it is our goal to provide education in a setting that is beneficial for the student. This book will give you the practical tool to create happy writers in a positive and hands-on environment.

Open up your heart and mind to transform the way you teach writing, regardless of the subjects you teach.

Are you ready to transform your young writers?

Happy Writing!

chapter one

The Writing Process and Writing Traits

"I forget what I taught. I only remember what I have learnt. "

Patrick White

WHY LEARNING THE WRITING PROCESS AND WRITING TRAITS IS IMPORTANT?

So many teachers, and teachers of writing, teach writing the best way they know, but why isn't it paying off when it comes to assessment?   Throughout my career as an elementary and secondary teacher and as a literacy coach, I have seen many changes in writing. When I first started teaching, I would put up on the board a story starter at least once a week and that was my one- draft story. I would then assign a topic around the theme we were studying in either science or social studies. I marked it up with corrections to spelling and conventions with my "red pencil" the student made a "good" copy and we would proceed to the next new writing piece.

Later, after taking several writing professional development courses, and learning a new awareness of the role of writing in literacy development , I realized the importance of the writing process, writing traits, and the writing workshop from such writing pioneers as Donald Graves,

Ruth Culham, Nancie Atwell, Lucy Calkins and Jane Hansen published books on "real writers techniques". These groundbreaking authors encourage teachers to use their writing ideas to teach writing.

Some of their researched-based writing practices are still hailed in high standards in teaching writing.

The writing process is how writing is generated it starts with:

- **Brainstorming** ~ Students list as many ideas about a particular subject as they can think of. This activity is led by the teacher, the whole class participates.
- **Prewriting** ~ Students planning before writing. Students write on topics based on their own

experiences. Students choose a graphic organizer appropriate for their composition based on genre and purpose. Students identify the audience for whom they will write.

- **Drafting** ~ Students write a rough draft or a "sloppy copy". Students emphasize content rather than mechanics.

- **Revising** ~ Students does not copy over or rewrite their writing piece. They share their writing in writing groups. Teachers are only concerned with the clarity, content, details and description in the writing. Teachers give feedback to students. Students make changes in their compositions to reflect the reactions and comments of teachers and classmates.

- **Editing ~** Students proofread their own writing. Students correct their own mechanical errors. Students meet with teacher for a final editing.
- **Publishing ~** Students complete the final copy of their writing. Students publish their own writing in an appropriate form. Students share their finished writing, sometimes in an author's chair.

The six steps of the writing process are vital to a writer's development and should be used consistently. All of the steps of the writing process are handy each time they write. Some other practices to consider during the writing process are using many techniques for response; including student-teacher conferences, peer review, class critiques, and self-assessments. Also, provide opportunities for students to collaborate as writers, thinkers, and learners by: Using collaboration techniques, modeling, providing checklist, and forms, and organizing small groups and writing pairs.

WRITING TRAITS:

When we read like a writer, we notice:

- **Ideas** ~ The writing piece's content. The two keys are clarity and details. Ideas and content focus on clear writing that presents details in an interesting manner.
- **Organization~** Is just the way it sounds, organizing a paper so it is easy for the reader to follow.

- **Voice** ~Is the author's fingerprint on the page. By using voice the reader feels more in touch with the writer's emotions, personality, and opinions. Voice is a favorite trait of students.

- **Word Choice~** The vocabulary the writer uses. This trait shows the power of language.

- **Sentence Fluency ~** Is a trait based solely on the ear. Students need to tune their ears to the rhythm, and cadence of the flow of words. Sentence variety helps attain fluency.

- **Conventions ~** The revising and editing component of writing. This trait is taught throughout the six traits writing process and is the most time consuming because of the depth and importance.

The most pivotal part of the writing classroom is the language of writers. All teachers of writing need to be on the same page and in the same lane when it comes to the terminology of writing. Teachers should use the appropriate terms when describing the writing process and the writing traits. The consistency of language among and between grades is an essential element of the writing curriculum.

chapter two

What are Mentor Texts? Why Use Them?

As teachers we all know that teaching writing is not the easiest thing to do, however, the writing process and writing traits are two big ideas we must understand and teach. Therefore, this is why I felt the need to write this book. This book hopefully will offer and easy guide to follow in assisting you teach writing continually every day.

One strategy I feel very passionate about is reading EVERY DAY to your students. One of the first books I can remember reading yearly to my primary grade students was the book "Did You Carry the Flag Today, Charley?" by Rebecca Caudill. I enjoyed the daily interaction with my students. This activity set a positive tone in my class for everything else we did from mathematics, science, and art. This is why I have a passion for reading to children a multiplicity of genres. Although, the term mentor text has a contemporary, professional stamp on it, to me it is just fantastic children's literature, or any text print or digital that you can read.

Using mentor text in the classroom to teach the writing process and writing traits is the most unique and timely solution for designing writing lessons. In their first book, *"Mentor Texts: Teaching Writing*

Through Children's Literature, K-6.", by Lynn R. Dorfman and Rose Capelli, these authors used mentor texts to develop writing strategies and lessons for professionals.

WHAT IS A MENTOR TEXT?

A mentor text is any text, print or digital, published by an author whose writing is studied in order to understand a writer's craft. The text can easily inspire students to write about a similar idea or to write with the same craft technique used by the author. Although, there are an abundance of mentor texts available, finding resources is not the most challenging part of the process, it is finding quality age appropriate, illustrated and non-illustrated text to teach specific writing skills and strategies. I have found that "practice does make perfect," you have to use a different mentor text over and over to start, then manipulate the text to fit the writing skills and traits. However, some good read aloud text are great for listening and some are better and make strong mentor texts for learning the author's craft.

"Reading aloud is linked with learning to write."

To emphasize, reading aloud is linked with learning to write. If elementary school teachers, especially, fail to read aloud to their students often, and regularly those students are going to be deprived of learning to write.

WHY USE MENTOR TEXTS?

We want our students to be more than proficient writers we want them to be great writers. Helping them find their writing voices and developing their craft using mentor text as a model is one reason why we use mentor text. Let me restate this important fact, as an educator we

"Help students find their writing voices."

need to use correct writing terms when communicating with our students during the writer's workshop.

Writing has the traits:

-Ideas

-Organization

-Voice

-Word Choice

-Sentence

-Fluency

-Conventions

"Good writing is EVERYWHERE."

These writing traits have to be taught and teachers need to routinely breakdown specific skills that students need to learn in order to write a strong writing piece.

Another reason, why we should use mentor text, is because good writing is everywhere and texts are readily available in your classroom, in the library, in print, digital and non-print resources. Finding your own mentor texts to enhance your teaching practice will generate lots of thinking, talking and writing that will inspire and motivate your students.

"*The writing you get out of your students can only be as good as the classroom literature that surrounds and sustains it.*"

Ralph Fletcher and Joann Portalupi,

Craft Lessons: Teaching Writing, K-8.

---

chapter three

Writing Workshop

WHAT IS A WRITER'S WORKSHOP?

An intense block of school time devoted to students planning, drafting, and editing writing for publication often involving peer collaboration. The structure of the workshop model includes four components:

- ✓ **Modeling**

- ✓ **Shared Writing**

- ✓ **Guided Writing**

- ✓ **Independent Writing**

Writing is a necessary and important area of literacy that supports comprehension, critical and creative thinking across content areas. My thirty-plus years of working with students and then seven years of working with teachers as a literacy coach has convinced me that the writing workshop gives all students the confidence and ability to become proficient writers by providing them with the very best tools, and these tools are provided by the teacher. As soon as, a teacher is ready to implement the writing workshop in the classroom, which should take place sometimes between the first and the fourth week of school, the teacher should set parameters.

First, it is very crucial that students have a time and space to write. At the same time, they need four or five days a week, from

45-minutes to an hour, to engage in the writing process.

These are a few essentials that can be implemented in the writing workshop: writing conferences, the writing cycle, writing traits, mentor texts,(using literature in writing), language skills, and editing checklists. The writing workshop allows teachers to meet the needs of their students by differentiating their instruction and improving instruction based on information obtain throughout the workshop.

In a writer's workshop, teachers set up the structure, allow students plenty of choices, and get them writing through continuous, repeated exposure to the writing cycle. It is a teaching technique that invites students to write by making the process a purposeful part of the classroom curriculum, and giving reading an integral role in the writing classroom," the reading-writing connection."

Let's Get Started!

BEGINNING A WRITING WORKSHOP IN YOUR CLASSROOM

- ✓ Begin by teaching students the stages of the writing process.
- ✓ Establish procedures for how a writing workshop will run in your classroom.
- ✓ Anticipate topics or mini-lessons that you will teach during the workshop. Usually these are lessons on new writings skills or language skills that students are misusing.

Decide how you will assess students' progress during writing workshop. Prepare checklists, organize schedules of observing students while they are writing, and create a grading rubric for the class so that all understand how the writing they produce during writing workshop will be graded.

Some suggestions for procedures and rules for writing workshops include:

- ✓ Students keep their writing in a designated place such as a writing folders or writer's notebook. Other important writing resource materials can be added to the folder later.
- ✓ Don't discard anything! All drafts, sloppy copies, jotting, drawings, show process and will be included in the final assessment of written work.
- ✓ Every piece of writing or entry in the writer's notebook or folder should be dated.
- ✓ All drafts should be written in pencil.
- ✓ Students should double space during

drafting so that revisions are easier to make.

✓ Use different color ink or crayon for revising and editing. For example, an **introduction**, can be circled in black, in an essay the student is writing, **idea one** can be underlined in red, **idea two** can be underlined in blue, and **idea three** can be underlined in green, and the **conclusion** can be boxed in black. Some additional parts of writing such as **similes, metaphors, and other figurative language** can be highlighted in yellow, **transitional words and phrases** can be underlined in purple, while **WOW words** (excellent choice of words) can be underlined in orange.

Mentor Text:

A mentor text is one that is written by an author and is shared with the class so that students can study that author's craft or style of writing. Usually the teacher reads aloud the text as a mentor text or writing style. If students are expected to practice and produce writing in these genres, then they need to be immersed with books based on those genres. These texts are known as mentor text.

Modeling:

During modeling time, the teacher demonstrates by writing on chart paper, chalkboard, and overhead/LCD. The teacher models aloud by thinking, rethinking, re-reading, and revising draft. The teacher talks aloud about topics such as: spacing needs, organizational patterns and transitional devices, and effective repetition. The teacher points out skills such as, spelling, punctuation, word choices, conventions, sentence structures, and revision techniques during the session.

Shared Writing:

During shared writing time, teacher and a class, compose aloud collaboratively. Both negotiate topics, purposes, and word choice.

The teacher acts as a scribe and encourages all students to participate. The teacher also provides explicit directions and questioning, encourages high-level thinking on focused, organization, support, and writer's craft.

Guided Writing:

Is when students write and the teacher guides. Explicit teaching is done in the form of mini lessons, for reinforcement of skills and introduction of new writer's craft lessons. Writing used during this time may be:

Responses to the literature, writing to learn and content areas, personal reflections, relating of information/reports.

In addition, guided practice provides an opportunity for teachers to work with groups of students or an individual student on effective writing strategies. The teacher's role is to confer with students or individuals on effective writing strategies and provide specific coaching based on students work and standards based rubrics.

The student's role is to confer with teacher and peers about the writing process and product. The student actively plans and constructs the texts, including editing. for a correct finished product.

Independent Writing:

In conclusion, Independent writing is when the students work alone, using their current knowledge of writing process, often choosing their own topics.

- ✓ Occurs daily in writer's workshop format.
- ✓ Teacher and students monitor through conference, and teacher feedback.
- ✓ Students will pick up on your passion,

your patience, and the persistence will make the writing workshop work well for you.

Sharing – "Author's Chair"

Writer's workshop ends with sharing in the "Author's Chair". This usually takes about five to ten minutes of time and can be done by either the students or teacher read to the class a "published piece" or by children sharing their work in pairs. Sharing is an extremely important component of the writing workshop that many teachers tend to dismiss due to time constraints of the day to day schedule. But this time is important because it gives students the opportunity to observe and learn from each other.

chapter four

Writing Modes

Even though everyone in education would somewhat agree that education is changing, and I hope for the better, in most states Common Core Standards are being taught. Whenever, the state adopts something new, there is always challenge and a push back from educators and parents. However, we must all unite to teach our children. Common Core Standards and state standards have integrated reading and writing in all subject areas, inspiring educators to refine their teaching strategies in both areas.

There are three writing modes, which are being used in the Common Core Standards; here are the definitions of those writing modes:

Narrative: The purpose of narrative writing is to write a personal or fictional experience, in an effective narration, where details work together and is easy to follow event sequences.

Expository/Informative/Explanatory: The purpose of informative writing is to inform, explain ideas, tells how to do something, how something works, writing that is clear and well organized, to support the main idea.

Persuasive/ Opinion: The purpose of opinion writing is to take a position for or against an issue, using relevant expertise and evidence to convince.

All of these writing modes drive the reasons students write in all subject areas and what they are writing. This is why mentor text is so important to use daily especially using nonfiction mentor text to enhance subject areas such as social studies, science, and mathematics.

Although, the 4W's of writing practices are writing process, writing traits, writing workshop, and writing modes are essential in teaching writing, they may be taught and understood separately, however, they should be taught as a coherent part of a complete instructional writing program/curriculum.

I have always used three of the 4W's daily in my writing plans. I fully support and encourage teachers to use this format frequently, at least three times a week, As students learn to write, it is critical that they analyze, visualize, discuss, and emulate a variety of writing models. When teaching any modes of writing, we must make it very clear to the students that the reason they are writing is to entertain, inform, or persuade, and that this is why authors write as well.

In order to gain confident writers in our classroom, we must Model and write in front of our students using writers' eyes. When teachers write for their students, it will help improve their own confidence and self-esteem. When we continually write for our students and ourselves, we immerse ourselves in the basics of writing craft and process. If the writing process is the "how" of exceptional writing, then the traits of writing is the "who". This Model allows us to focus on the most important and indispensable form of modeling, including mentor texts, quality literature and student writing models.

Teachers should model first, the strategies they want their students to use in their own writing as many times as necessary, and find mentor texts where the author's purpose and strategy is clear. Teachers do not have to read aloud the entire book or chapter of a novel, to emphasize a writing strategy or skill. Fiction and Nonfiction texts can be used in the elementary classroom grades to help students understand strategies needed for all writing modes.

chapter five

Narrative Writing: Using Mentor Texts

The ultimate purpose of this book is to help students become effective writers and teachers become excellent teachers of writing that focus on fiction and nonfiction mentor texts. The quote by Marcia S. Freeman expresses my thought about writers. "All writers need time to think and talk about their ideas...Talking helps writers focus their idea and discover how they want to present it."

In this chapter and the next two chapters I chose nine mini lessons over three genres of writing to share. These mini lessons were taught in the elementary grade classroom. All of these mini lessons are effective practices in literacy instruction. The mini lessons are classroom tested and proven to improve student learning gains and writing instructions. The script in each mini lesson can be modified to fit every elementary classroom. Although, some mini lessons are grade specific, and some writing skills fit better with specific genres, the mini lessons are developmentally appropriate to be used in all elementary classrooms.

The mini lessons were developed around the structure of the writing workshop and the writing traits. Teachers can peruse each mini lesson to make the decisions about the lesson that suits the writing learning needs of their students. If the students are to master the writing objective of the lesson, then the lesson needs to be taught more than once. I suggest using a different mentor text when you repeat a lesson.

The mini lessons are based on effective lesson plans. The mini lesson has several teaching components, which include: Objective, Instructions, and Independent Practices. The lesson objective help provide what students are going to learn in the mini lesson. The instruction is the modeling phase, where the explicit and direct teaching is demonstrated. The last component is the independent practice where students are given the opportunity to demonstrate what they have learned. Some lessons also include extensions, which are suggestions for applying the lesson further.

MINI LESSONS
for *Narrative Writing*

Lesson #1
Choosing the Right Lead/ Beginning
(Grades 3-6)

Lesson #2
Identifying the Beginning, Middle and
Ending of a Story
(Grades 1-3)

Lesson #3
"Show, Don't Tell"
(Grades 1-3)

**Mini Lessons
for Narrative Writing #1**

Choosing the Right Lead/ Beginning (Grades 3-6)

Mentor Texts:

Superfudge by Judy Blume

Widget by Lyn Rossiter McFarland

The Watsons Go To Birmingham-1963

by Christopher Paul Curtis

Too Many Tamales by Gary Soto

Charlotte's Web by E.B.White

Objective: Students will be able to identify four main "leads" in literature.

Instructions: Use the suggested mentor texts or a variety of books of your choice. Read the first line or two from each one. Explain to the students that one way to capture the reader's attention in a writing piece is to write a great lead sentence. Focus on the types of leads used. For example: Onomatopoeia, Opinion, Specific statement, and Dialogue. All students in the group discuss what type of "lead" was read aloud by the teacher. The teacher chooses about ten to fifteen mentor text to be used, five in each location, with different leads in each mentor textbook.

Independent Practice: Tell the students talking is not allowed. Students rotate at the directions of the teacher to begin working, and writing down the first sentence in each of the books. After 20 minutes rotate group. This mini lesson can be completed in two 40 minute sessions. At the end of the sessions have the students volunteer to share and the identify the "leads".

Extension: Tell the students that in pairs, they will create two new "leads" for the mentor texts used,(borrow from the author's sentence structure, the lead-the first sentence, the first paragraph, or the first several paragraphs that begins the story). For example: If the text uses a "lead" built around describing the character, encourage the pairs to create a lead that uses another strategy such as dialogue.

Trait: Organization

Notes

Mini Lessons for Narrative Writing #2

Identifying the Beginning, Middle and Ending of a Story
(Grades 1-3)

Mentor Texts:

Amazing Grace by Mary Hoffman

Lily's Purple Plastic Purse by Kevin Henkes

Crab Moon by Ruth Horowitz

*Where the Wild Things Are by Maurice Sendak

Shortcut by Donald Crews

Objective: Students will identify the beginning, middle, and end of a story. Students will write or draw a story with a beginning, middle and end.

Instructions: Read the story aloud. Have the students retell the story. The starred mentor text book is used in this mini lesson. Discuss what happened at the beginning, middle and end. Model thinking aloud to show students how you determine the beginning, middle, and end. Put students in small groups. Pass out one set of sentence strips per group/table.(The BME sentences for the sentence strip will be at the end of the mini lesson), the sentence strips can be placed on the board and discuss the correct order. Read each sentence strip and show it to the class.

Have them determine the correct order for each sentence strip.(BME)

Independent Practice: Have students draw three illustrations that demonstrate the beginning, middle, and end of the story. This will probably take two to three days. If your students are able to write a story with the beginning, middle and end and circle each section with a different color crayon. The beginning can be circled in red, the middle in blue and the end in green.

Sentences to be written on the sentence strips.

Max was acting like a wolf and was sent to his room for misbehaving.
Max travels to the land of the wild things to become their king.

Max feels lonely and returns home to find his hot supper waiting.

Trait: Organization

Notes

**Mini Lessons
for Narrative Writing #3**

Inspire Me!

"Show, Don't Tell" (Grades 1-3)

Mentor Texts:

The Other Way To Listen by Byrd Baylor

When I was Young in the Mountain by Cynthia Rylant

The Purple Coat by Amy Hest

The Polar Express by Chris Van Allsburg

Objective: To use descriptive details in showing not telling in writing.

Instruction: Show and discuss with students the sentence, "The flower is beautiful" tell them we want to show the reader what the sentence means. Then, show and discuss the sentence with a more explicit detail, "The flower has deep blue petals and green leaves." This mini lesson is intended to help make the concept of showing more explicit and to provide students with practice in revising their writing. Brainstorm with the students the description of their favorite sandwich and how to make it. Then, create a text with the brainstorm ideas.

My favorite sandwiches are hot dogs and there are three steps in making the perfect dog: getting out the food, cooking the hot dogs and bun, and putting it all together with my favorite goodies.

Independent Practice: Have students practice the "Show, Don't Tell" activity in pairs. Give each pair of students a sentence and have them write several descriptions that "show."

The practice for this lesson appears in the writing resource section of this book.

-Eating a piece of pizza

-He is a very good friend

-Kicking a soccer ball

-The student was rude to the teacher

-The gerbil got away

-She has a messy room

Trait: Word Choice

Notes

Notes

chapter six

Informational/Expository Writing: Using Nonfiction Mentor Texts

---

"Write what makes you happy; there is no other rule."

-O. Henry

Personally for me, I enjoy reading and especially writing nonfiction informational writing. I embrace the idea to write about ordinary things in an extraordinary way. Writing is a difficult task that comprises a large range of abilities, making it one of the most challenging to teach. In the same way that authors write, to entertain, inform and to persuade, or to decide what ideas to include, choose appropriate words, putting the text in a logical order. This is what everyone must consider when writing, even our children. Those are daunting facts and skills!!!

The ability to write informational writing effectively is greater today than ever. Over seventy-five percent of all materials that are written, available or published in digital form on the Internet are nonfiction.

WHAT IS INFORMATIONAL WRITING?

Informational writing is nonfiction. As a literacy coach, I emphasized to students to look for key words in informational writing such as explain, define, clarify, inform and instruct. Today, if you think of informational writing it is to relay facts and information in a cohesive and thoughtful way. However, it does not mean that it is not fascinating and fun to read or write.

Some of the best stories I shared with my students were nonfiction. The Common Core Standards (NGA Center & CCSSO, 2010) defines it —"to examine and convey information accurately." "To produce this kind of writing, students draw from what they already know and from primary and secondary sources." This writing differs from narrative text in its structure, content, and functions, because often with information from several sources you must use fluency to form a cohesive whole.

There are two main categories of informational writing, they are descriptive and informative. This is where the writing traits are presented. Usually descriptive writing relates information in a way that creates sensory perceptions. Although, descriptive writing builds images in the readers mind, it is a component of other genres. Informative writing presents intriguing facts that shows how much the writer really knows and has thought about the idea.

Informational writing includes a wide array of essays, charts, graphs, advice columns, biographies; magazine articles just to name a few. In addition, thousands of web sites present information in several formats. All good informational writing follows a pattern. First, the main idea must be clearly stated, or implied. It must be clearly established. The main idea must be supported by relevant facts that are valid. These facts must be presented in a logical, organized, and clear structure. When students carefully consider the pattern and structure used in their writing piece they will immediately identify their writing as *Good Writing*.

In Chapter 7, Persuasive/Opinion Writing is a discussion on arguments used to change the reader's point of view. The quote, "Practice safe eating- always use condiments." Exemplifies what the next area of writing is about. Adding the condiments to the food, (the other writing genres) we have supplied our students with to take them to next academic level, be it college or career.

Finding a Topic: Grades 1-6

Mini Lesson

Mentor Texts and the Idea traits.

Objective: Who?, What?, When?, Where?, Why?

Instructions: This sign cautions shoppers in a parking lot of a metropolitan city mall, to take precautions to be safe.

Students can write their narrative about this sign and why they are helpful to keeping shoppers safe.

Independent Practice: Explore the 5W's.

Notes

MINI LESSONS
for
Informational/ Expository Writing

Inspire Me!

Lesson #1
Using Descriptive Writing
(Grades 1-2)

Lesson #2
Getting Pumped Up with
Informational Writing
(Grades 4-6)

Lesson #3
Using Similes, Metaphors
and Idioms to Teach
(Grades 3-6) ~ Figurative Language

Mini Lessons for Informational/ Expository Writing #1

Inspire Me!

Using Descriptive Writing (Grades 1-2)

Nonfiction Mentor Texts:

Crab Moon by Ruth Horowitz

One Giant Leap by Robert Burleigh

Stellaluna by Janell Cannon

Trait: Word Choice

Objectives: Students will demonstrate their understanding of word choice by writing with descriptive words.

Instructions: Read aloud the book <u>Crab Moon</u> by Ruth Horowitz. Display five large pieces of chart paper labeled with illustrations of: sight, touch, taste, hearing, and smell. Use these chart to help introduce sensory words to your students. Reread the story, a page at a time, having students help with identifying words used with the five senses. Record the words on the chart paper. Demonstrate how to use descriptive words by filling in the blanks in <u>one</u> of the paragraphs below.

Paragraph #1

The_____ Daniel turned _____ his _____ rented a cottage at the _____. They arrived on the _____ of the full moon.

Paragraph #2

"The _____ moon in _____ brings the _____tide of the horseshoe crabs," said his _____. "I saw them laying their _____ on this _____ when I was your age."

Paragraph #3

"Every_____," his mother answered. "Horseshoe crabs have been coming _____ for _____of millions of years. They're older than the _____.

Independent Practice:

Students can work with partners to fill in the second paragraph, then assign the final paragraph as independent practice.

Notes

Mini Lessons for Informational/ Expository Writing #2

Getting Pumped Up with Informational Writing
(Grades 4-6)

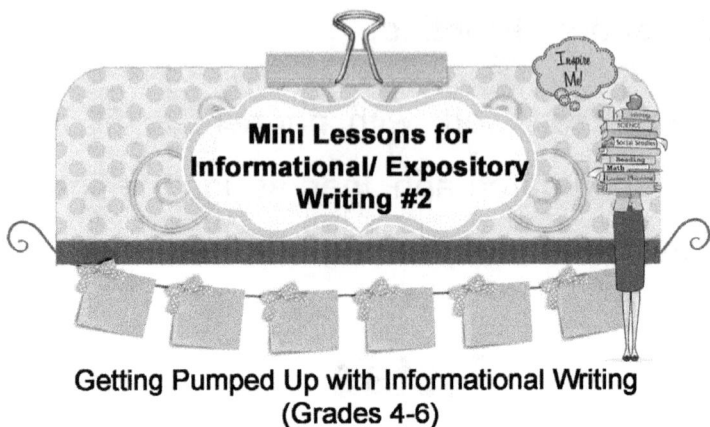

Nonfiction Mentor Texts:

Beacon Light: Lighthouses by Gail Gibbons

Lightning by Stephen Kramer

Sharks by Gary Lopez

Objectives: Students will be able to use an identify voice in their informational writing.

Examples of Pumped Up Writing: *Using similes or metaphors, colorful descriptions, and examples or anecdote, humor, and a personal experience or connection.*

Instructions: Read aloud the passage from <u>Beacons Light: Lighthouses</u> by Gail Gibbon, or passage from any of the suggested nonfiction mentor books, or any science textbook of your grade level. Let the students know that informational writing is often used to educate or inform but that does not mean it has to be boring or dull. Let the students see how to use some of the facts collected to create a Pumped Up introduction. Then use the short passages below for modeling in front of the students.

After reading it aloud, list some of the facts from the passage on the board. Then create an example from Pumped Up Writing. When you think the students are ready, have them return to the passages. Have them partner up for sharing. This mini lesson will have to be taught frequently to enhance this skill.

Trait: Voice

Passage #1

Beacons of Light: Lighthouses by Gail Gibbons

Waves thrash and winds swirl, tossing a ship about in the darkness. Then, in the distance, a light appears. It flashes three times, disappears, then flashes again. On board, the ship's crew recognizes that this is a lighthouse signal. It is telling them to veer away from something hidden beneath the water. The captain locates a rocky ledge on his chart and uses the light signal to plot their position.

Passage #2

Sharks by Gary Lopez

The ocean water is clear and blue in the

bright sunshine. Under the surface, schools of colorful fish swim through the water. Among them swims a sleek animal with a long tail and very sharp teeth. This animal is cruising through the water looking for its next meal. People all over the world fear this creature. What is it? It's a shark!

Passage #3

Lightning by Stephen Kramer

Late in the evening, a dark cloud hangs in the sky. The air is calm. The birds are quiet. Even the blades of dry grass are still. Everything is hushed, waiting. Suddenly a giant spark leaps through the air, connecting earth and sky. The spark flickers for and instant and disappears. There is a moment of silence. Then a tremendous CRACK rips through the quiet.

Booming echoes follow, rolling across the land. A thunderstorm drifts across the summer sky.

Notes

Notes

Mini Lessons for Informational/ Expository Writing #3

Using Similes, Metaphors and Idioms to Teach
(Grades 3-6) ~ Figurative Language

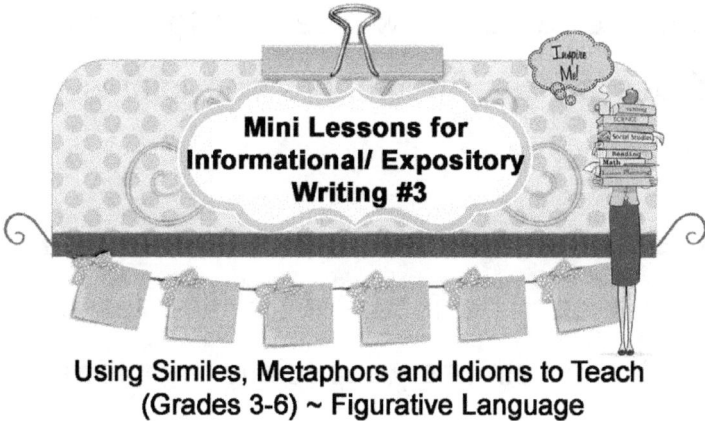

Nonfiction Mentor Texts:

There is a Frog in My Throat by Loreen Leedy and Pat Street

Owl Moon by Jane Yolen

The Ocean Is by Kathleen Kranking

Sky Boys: How they Built The Empire State Building by Deborah Hopkinson

*In A Pickle and other Funny Idioms by Marvin Terban

Objective: Students will be able to identify and use similes, metaphors and idioms in their writing.

Instructions: Choose any of the mentor text to read. The focus of the first lesson should be similes especially in lower elementary, or to reinforce the skill. The book, In A Pickle, and other Funny Idioms by Marvin Terban, is an excellent text to use to introduce metaphors and idioms. Choose a metaphor or an idiom to model. One of my favorites, "Your Eyes Are Bigger Than Your Stomach." I showed the students a non-literal meaning of the phrase using a picture from the mentor text and then I discussed the literal meaning of the phrase followed by an example of how I once went out to a restaurant with a friend and she ordered a full four course meal because she thought she could eat it all. She realized what it meant, "Your eyes are bigger than your stomach."

Independent Practice: From a list of metaphors and idioms that can be placed on the board, on a chart, in the student's writing notebook, students will practice with a partner writing four different metaphors and/or idioms from the list, each partner working with two different metaphors or idioms. The students will illustrate the non-literal meaning of the idiom/ metaphor and write the literal meaning of the metaphor/idiom.

The purpose of this activity is to show ways to add flavor and flair to their writing using figurative language. You will find a metaphors and idioms list in the writing resource chapter of this book that is quite

helpful and useful to use with this lesson.

Notes

chapter seven

Persuasive /Opinion Writing: Using Mentor Texts

Persuasive writing is defined as presenting reasons and examples to influence action or thought, requiring the writer to state clearly an opinion and to supply reasons and specific examples that support the opinion. As students mature as writers it is very important to give them the opportunity to write using a variety of formats. Persuasive writing helps students formulate specific reasons for their opinions and provide opportunity to research facts related to their opinion. At this point, we have discussed two of the three genres of writing. As teachers, we are preparing our students for college and careers. We should still put great emphasis on persuasive writing even though Common Core State Standards in English Language Arts are being used in most states.

Student writers will now have to do more direct writing using the Argument genre rather than the persuasive genre. However, student writers will need more instructions in writing arguments. In most elementary classrooms, the main focus of writing for the school year is narrative and informal writing. Teachers will have to explore creative ways for students to write strong opinion position papers. I will provide you a list of mentor texts and persuasive writing prompts to use with Persuasive/Opinion

Writing.

As I mentioned earlier, every teacher should be a teacher of writing, especially nonfiction/ informational writing, which should be integrated into every subject area. My goal as an educator is to help each student communicate their thoughts clear and concise through writing the point they want to make. This book is the step in that direction that will provide the teachers with the tools and ideas for crafting writing in their classrooms.

Persuasive/Opinion Texts:

- **<u>Team Moon: How 400,000 People Landed Apollo 11 on the Moon</u>** by Catherine Thimmesh
- **<u>Harvest Year</u>** by Cris Peterson
- **<u>The Journey: Stories of Migration</u>** by Cynthia Rylant
- **<u>Penny: The forgotten Coin</u>** by Denise Brennan-Nelson
- **<u>Talkin' About Bessie: The Story of Aviator Elizabeth Coleman</u>** by Nikki Grimes
- **<u>My Brother Dan's Delicious</u>** by Steven Layne
- **<u>The Important Book</u>** by Margaret Wise
- **<u>Click, Clack, Moo: Cows that Type</u>** by Doreen Cronin

- **Teammates** by Peter Golenbock
- **Dear Mrs. LaRue: Letters from Obedience School** by Mark Teague
- **Almost Gone: The World's Rarest Animals** by Steve Jenkins
- **From Slave Ship to Freedom Road** by Julius Lester
- **Please Don't Wake the Animals: A Book About Sleep** by Mary Batten
- **Rain Forest** by Angela Wilkes

The Common Core State Standards for English Language Arts has a key shift in the standards, which are essential, one of the shifts involve building knowledge through content-rich nonfiction. The list above meets the criteria for informational text building student's content knowledge.

PERSUASIVE ESSAYS

Objective:

- The student will develop critical thinking skills by analyzing, and evaluating various sides of an issue to form a conclusion.
- Work cooperatively in groups
- Compare and Contrast, drawing conclusion, examining different viewpoints

Prompt: Write a Persuasive Essay to argue <u>for or against</u> the following idea:

Abandoned pets should be put to sleep at the Animal Shelter.

Prompt: Write a Persuasive Essay to argue <u>for or against</u> the following idea:

Should Kids Under age 10 years old have Cell Phones at school?

Prompt: Some people think kids should not watch television on school nights. Do you think this is a good idea for parents to agree or disagree with? Write three reasons why you would try to persuade your parents to agree or disagree with your opinion.

Prompt: Many people like to plant gardens in the spring. First Lady Michelle Obama broke ground at the White House to plant crops on the South lawn. She and some fifth graders planted spinach, broccoli, blueberries and various other fruits and vegetables. Write to persuade your parents that you would like to start a garden and about the kinds of things you would like to plant there and the reasons why?

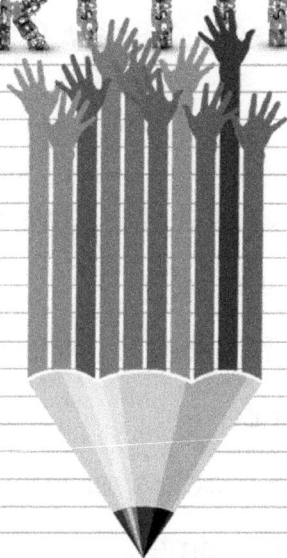

RESOURCES

Persuasive Essay Organizer

Narrative Graphic Organizer

Expository Graphic Organizers

Model how to Address a Prompt

List of Metaphors and Idioms

"Show, Don't Tell" Practice

Persuasive Essay Organizer

- Introduces the writer's position with a thesis statement
- Supports the position with reasons and evidence
- Appeals to readers' emotions without sounding extreme
- Acknowledges opposing points of view
- Ends with a call to action.

In the chart, gather facts and details to support your argument. You might include personal examples, facts, statistics, and experts' opinions.

Argument	Evidence

Organize your main supporting points in order of importance.

POSITION:

Reason 1:

Reason 2:

Reason 3:

Narrative Graphic Organizer

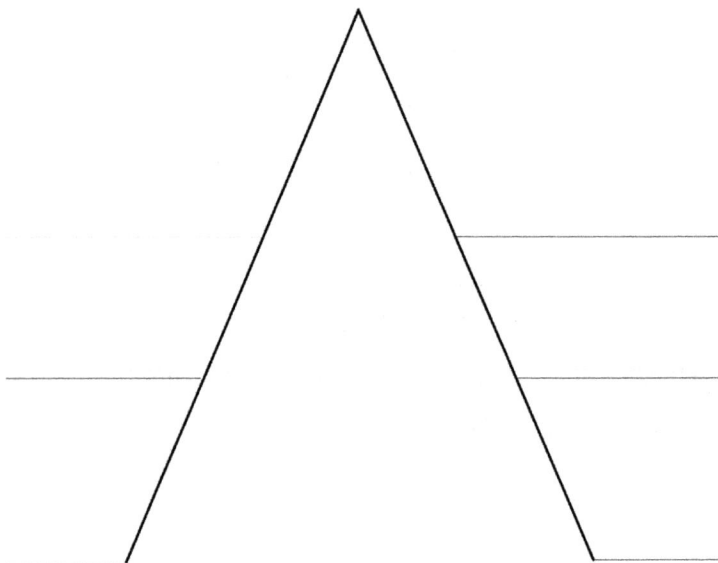

When:
Who:
Where:
Problem:

When:
Who:
Where:
Just remember..

Expository Graphic Organizers

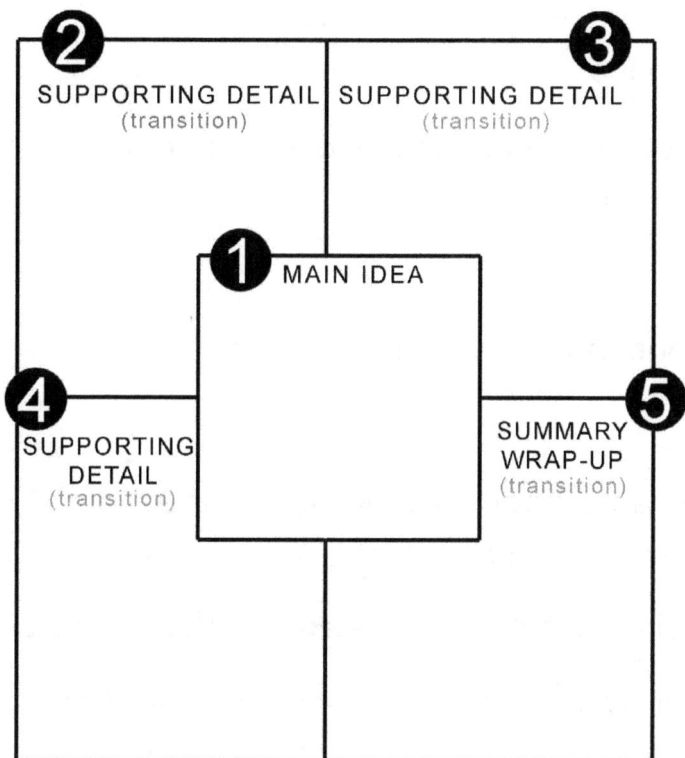

2 SUPPORTING DETAIL
(transition)

3 SUPPORTING DETAIL
(transition)

1 MAIN IDEA

4 SUPPORTING
DETAIL
(transition)

5 SUMMARY
WRAP-UP
(transition)

Model How to Address a Prompt

First, read each prompt.

Decide if the prompt is expository or narrative.

Follow the directions below to address each prompt.

*Model how to address a prompt:

1. Draw a happy face ☺ next to the topic. (first sentence)

2. Circle what you are asked to think about.

3. Draw a rectangle around the word that lets you know that it is a narrative or expository prompt.

4. Underline the rest of the sentence. (What you are supposed to write about or explain), which is usually the last part.

What do you like most about school?

Think about what you like most about school.

Now write to explain what you like most about school.

FL DOE 4th Gr. Prompt, 2014.

Animals sometimes surprise us by doing something smart.

Think about a time an animal did something smart.

Now write a story about the time an animal did something smart.

Everyone has had a day he or she had a happy memory.

Before you begin writing, think about a time that you were happy.

Now write to explain to the reader of your paper what made you happy.

List of Metaphors and Idioms

An accident waiting to happen

Apple of one's eye

Beat around the bush

Blows me away

Butterflies in your stomach

Cold feet

Cool

Cost an arm and a leg

Devil's advocate

Don't put all your eggs in one basket

Down in the dumps

Eyes are bigger than your stomach

Feeling under the weather

He's a pain in the neck

I'm broke

I'm in a pickle

I held my tongue

It's a piece a cake

Let the cat out of the bag

Money burns a hole in his pocket

Off the chain

On pins and needles

On the right track

Praise the bridge that takes you safely across

Raining cats and dogs

Spitting image

The light of my life

Tie the knot

To rub someone the wrong way

Wet behind the ears

"Show, Don't Tell" Practice

She has a messy room.

Eating a piece of pizza

Kicking a soccer ball

The gerbil got away

references

1. Capelli, Rose & Dorfman, Lynn R. *Mentor Texts: Teaching Writing Through Children's Literature, K-6 (2007)*

2. Capelli, Rose & Dorfman, Lynn R. *Nonfiction Mentor Texts: Teaching Informational Writing Through Children's Literature,K-8 (2009)*

3. Culham, Ruth, *The Writing Thief- Using Mentor Texts to teach the Craft of Writing (2014)*

4. Fletcher, R.,& Portalupi, J., *Nonfiction Craft Lessons: Teaching Information Writing K-8 (2001)*

Francina
Mainer

FOR YOUR NEXT EVENT

Speaker
Independent Consultant
Writing Coach
(Writing, Language Arts, Reading)
Private Tutoring

www.FrancinaMainer.com

ABOUT THE AUTHOR

Francina Mainer an experienced Writing Coach who is passionate about empowering others through the craft of writing. She has taught Elementary and Secondary Education for over thirty years in Florida and Georgia. Francina Mainer received a B.A. from University of South Florida, Tampa, FL, in Early Childhood and Elementary Education, and a M.Ed. from Nova Southeastern University, Fort Lauderdale, FL, in Education with an emphasis in Reading and Writing/Language Arts. She has also spent seven years as a literacy coach in public school.

As a life-long learner, she has attended a multiplicity of professional workshops throughout her career and still is active in several professional organizations. Francina Mainer is currently certified in K-6 Early Childhood & Elementary Education, Middle Grade English, ESOL, Gifted and Reading endorsed.

She resides in Orlando, Florida, has two adult children, and one grand child. Francina loves to travel and enjoys reading, writing and listening to great music.